Sharing Our Yard

Written by Marilyn Woolley
Series Consultant: Linda Hoyt

WorldWise™
Content-based Learning

Contents

Introduction

Anna and her family live in North Queensland, Australia. They like to study animals that live near or visit their yard. They work with scientists to make sure that the animals' **habitats** will be safe in the future.

Anna's favourite animals are the Ulysses blue butterfly, the crimson finch and the musky rat-kangaroo.

Chapter 1

The Ulysses blue butterfly

The Ulysses blue butterfly visits Anna's yard all year long because the plants it needs grow there. It feeds on the pink flowers of the corkwood tree and gets its food from the flower's **nectar**. The butterfly lays its eggs on this tree's leaves, and the caterpillar feeds on these leaves.

Life cycle of the Ulysses blue butterfly

Female butterfly lays eggs on corkwood tree leaf.

One week later
Eggs hatch, and caterpillars feed on corkwood leaves. They shed their skin several times as they grow.

New cycle begins as adults mate.

Each caterpillar builds a **chrysalis** and changes into a butterfly.

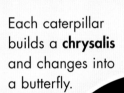

After two weeks
Adult butterflies emerge and feed on the flowers of the corkwood tree.

In the past, rainforest trees were destroyed as people cut them down to plant sugar cane. Ulysses blue butterflies could not get food or find a place to lay their eggs. Lots of butterflies died. So few were left that they were listed as **protected**.

People in North Queensland planted corkwood trees in their yards to bring back the butterflies. Anna and her mum grew corkwood trees in their yard, too.

Soon, the butterflies started to come back to these trees. They laid their eggs. The young caterpillars could eat the corkwood leaves, and the adults fed on the nectar of the corkwood flower.

The flowers of the corkwood tree

Protecting the Ulysses blue butterfly

This butterfly's natural habitat is managed and protected. Scientists are studying this butterfly, and butterfly zoos have programs to breed Ulysses blue butterflies to release into the wild.

Ulysses blue butterfly at the Australian Butterfly Sanctuary

Chapter 2

The crimson finch

There are very few crimson finches in North Queensland because people have cut down the birds' nesting trees. These birds eat grass seeds, and bushfires and weeds have destroyed places where grasses grow.

Anna and her mum help protect the crimson finch. They planted a pandanus tree in their backyard and grew **native** grasses underneath it. They know that crimson finches build their nests in the palms and eat native grass seeds.

Anna and her mum also know that finches drink fresh water so they put out clean water in a birdbath.

Did you know?

These tiny birds land on the stem of native grasses, and pluck the seeds from the seed-heads or eat the seeds that fall to the ground.

▼ The crimson finch eats the seeds of this native grass.

▼ The pandanus tree in Anna's yard

As the pandanus tree grew bigger, two crimson finches came to Anna's yard. They used grasses and bits of bark to build a nest in the fronds of this tree. Both parents took turns to sit on the eggs.

After two weeks, Anna saw the heads of six young finches in the nest. Both parents fed these young.

Find out more
How long do young crimson finches stay in the nest?

Chapter 3

The musky rat-kangaroo

Near where Anna lives, there is an area to protect the musky rat-kangaroo. Anna and her family often visit this area to study what the rat-kangaroos are eating or doing. This **marsupial** is only found in a small area of rainforest in Queensland.

Did you know?

The musky rat-kangaroo uses its long, thin tail to carry a bundle of dry leaves, ferns and twigs to make its nest in a vine.

The musky rat-kangaroo is much smaller than other kangaroos. It bounds like a rabbit on its four legs. During the day, the musky rat-kangaroo **forages** on the forest floor for fruit and insects. It makes a nest, where it rests in the middle of the day and at night.

The musky rat-kangaroo has two babies that it carries in its pouch and feeds on milk. In October, the young leave the pouch to eat the fruit on the forest floor.

Musky rat-kangaroos bury some fruit to eat later. Some of the seeds grow into new rainforest trees.

Some people want to cut down the rainforest trees for **timber**. Others, like Anna and her mum, try to set up **protected** areas to save the rainforest trees so that the musky rat-kangaroo can shelter and find enough food.

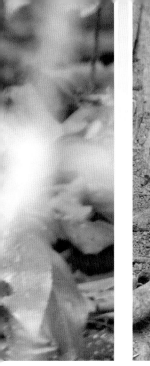

The musky rat-kangaroo eats the red fruit of the king palm, when it falls on the forest floor.

Conclusion

These three animals are important in North Queensland. They need safe places to raise their young, to shelter when it is very hot or to hide from **predators**. Many people now make sure that the right kind of plants and clean water are in their yards for these animals. They work with others to set aside **protected** areas for them, too.

Glossary

chrysalis the hard outer case that has a caterpillar inside turning into an adult

forages searches for food

habitats the places where a plant or an animal lives

marsupial a type of animal that carries its babies in a pocket of skin on the mother's stomach

native living naturally in an area

nectar a sweet liquid that plants make

predators animals that get food by killing and eating other animals

protected cannot be harmed

timber wood that is used for building

Index